S0-AXR-263

Ten Steps to Victory Over Depression

Tim LaHaye

Ten Steps to Victory Over Depression

from
"How to Win Over Depression"

ZONDERVAN
PUBLISHING HOUSE
OF THE ZONDERVAN CORPORATION | GRAND RAPIDS, MICHIGAN 49506

TEN STEPS TO VICTORY OVER DEPRESSION
is excerpted from
How to Win Over Depression

Copyright © 1974 by The Zondervan Corporation
Grand Rapids, Michigan

Library of Congress Catalog Card Number 73-22692

Twelfth printing 1980
ISBN 0-310-27002-2

Printed in the United States of America

A Word From the Author . . .

How to Win Over Depression, the book from which this booklet was excerpted, has been widely received and acclaimed. Hundreds have written indicating that they were helped by it and others have found Christ as a result of reading the book. Recently a man spoke to me at a wedding. He had received the book three months ago and had been converted. His family was saved, too, and they sent for some tapes to listen to in their home. They invited some friends in and two family friends have since received Christ. I've also had reports of Bible classes using *How to Win Over Depression* as a study book. All of this is very gratifying to me and I pray God will use this little excerpt in an even wider ministry of healing.

INTRODUCTION

An attractive woman in her mid-thirties sat in my counseling room and heaved that long and somewhat discouraging sigh I had come to associate with the depressed. Her name could have been "Mrs. Everything" — you name it, she had it.

Leaving her $65,000 ranch-style home and a wardrobe filled with mod clothes, she drove her troubles to my office in a new station wagon. She had three lovely school-age daughters and a dynamic executive-type husband who had "never been unfaithful." Even though she possessed almost everything she wanted, she was not happy.

Three times a week for two months she had been seeing a psychiatrist, yet only two nights before coming to me Mrs. Everything had almost taken her life. In a state of depression she had lowered the shades in her bedroom, had crawled back into bed as soon as the girls had left for school, and had pulled the sheets up over her head. Her well-groomed appearance to the contrary, she claimed that she had climbed out of such a bed to visit my office.

Although that young mother's case of depression was severe, it was not the worst I had ever seen. In fact, her emotional condition was not at all uncommon, for the majority of people I counsel are depressed. In talking to other counselors, I find this to be the general rule. On almost any day the average counselor is confronted with several cases of depression. A prominent psychologist recently observed, "Every one of us is depressed at times. It is perfectly normal." A medical doctor, lecturing to other doctors on how to diagnose depression, commented, "In a sense, depression should be expected in every individual."

For many years depression has been the nation's number one emotional illness and it is on the increase. At more than 75 Family Life Seminars I have conducted in various parts of the country, my cassette lecture on "The Cause and Cure of Depression" has without exception sold more than any other lecture — even more than "Sexual Harmony in Marriage," "Overcoming Worry," "Why Opposites Attract Each other," and ten other selections.

Between 50,000 and 70,000 people commit suicide each year, and we know that only a small percent of those who attempt suicide actually succeed. Investigation has revealed that more than half of these people were suffering from depression. The National Institute of Mental Health indicates that 125,000 Americans are hospitalized annually with depression, whereas another 200,000 or more are treated by psychiatrists. Dr. Nathan Kline of New York's Rockland State Hospital reports that many unrecognized cases of depression go untreated. Estimates reach as high as four to eight million annually. In the opinion of many researchers, more human suffering results from depression than from any other disease affecting mankind.

Even *Newsweek* magazine devoted its front cover and lead article to "Coping with Depression"

(Jan. 8, 1973) in which the author stated, "There is no doubt that depression, long the leading mental illness in the United States is now virtually epidemic, and suicide is its all too frequent outcome." During the past few years, I have taken polls in audiences totaling at least 200,000 people, inquiring, "Is there anyone here who has never experienced depression in his entire life?" So far not one person has indicated that he has escaped this problem. Truly it can be said to one degree or another, depression is universal.

Ten
Steps
to Victory
Over
Depression

Ten Steps to Victory Over Depression

A twenty-four-year-old woman who came in for counseling acknowledged many years of depression. During the preceding four years she had undergone thirty electric shock treatments for the malady — and was nothing bettered. In fact, her problem was compounded by a loss of memory. She had lost at least two years of her life in sanitariums due to depression.

Looking into the face of this attractive young woman, I couldn't help thinking how her case was so typical of the severely depressed. To begin with, she was predominantly melancholy in temperament; consequently she was negative, sensitive and overly occupied with herself. In addition, she had lost all hope for the future. The product of a broken home, she was literally unwanted by either parent or her brothers and sisters.

The first step in Beth's remarkable recovery was taken when she accepted Jesus Christ as her personal Lord and Savior. He provided the assurance of love and forgiveness she had always longed for. He also provided her with the power to overcome her thought patterns of resentment and self-pity. By gaining the ability from Him to forgive her parents, she removed the root of bitterness that had immobilized her for years.

Three months after her conversion she discontinued the drugs prescribed by her psychiatrist and experienced the best emotional stability of her life. She revisited her psychiatrist at our suggestion, because she felt guilty at not formally terminating her treatments. He was overjoyed at the change in his patient and immediately jumped to the conclusion that his combination of drug therapy and psychotherapy had finally brought her relief. When she informed him that she had become a Christian and that Christ had brought a whole new way of life to her, it must have been a threat to him, for he immediately lashed out at her in a most unprofessional manner. He warned her that "it will not last! Christianity is only a crutch; you will be back here in a few weeks worse off than you were before." She informed him that she was no longer taking his drugs and was sleeping better than ever. He berated both her faith and her intelligence.

Fortunately, Beth drove straight to my office. All she needed was some biblical reassurance to the reality of her experience. We once again reviewed the steps to overcoming depression that had already helped her. Gradually her confidence and joy returned, and she left my office to continue living that abundant Christian life the Lord has promised to all His children who meet His conditions. If her experience with Christ is only a "crutch," it must be a pretty good one, because it has been almost a year now since she has been depressed, in spite of the fact that her family circumstances and living conditions have actually gotten worse.

Your depression, or that of someone you love, that has caused you to read this booklet is probably not nearly as severe as was Beth's. These five preliminary steps to victory over depression that have proven so effective for her will prove equally beneficial to you if you use them.

(a) *Accept Jesus Christ as your Savior* — With all due respect to the powers of your mind and will, you do not have the capacity to avoid depression without help from God. One of the tragic blunders of modern psychology, success motivation, or other humanistic forms of self-improvement lies in its presumption that man does not need God's help to lift him out of depression. Jesus Christ said, ". . . without me ye can do nothing" (John 15:5), and this is particularly true of depression. If you anticipate victory over depression on a lasting basis, you must begin by inviting Jesus Christ into your life. Once you have done that you will then possess the divine resources of God to enable you to take the next nine steps for victory over depression. If you are not sure you have had such an experience, I would counsel you first of all to slip to your knees and personally invite Him into your life. Be assured of the promise,

"For whosoever shall call upon the name of the Lord shall be saved" (Rom. 10:13).

(b) *Walk in the Spirit* — Accepting Jesus Christ as your personal Savior and walking in the Spirit on a day-to-day basis are not identical experiences. The latter, of course, is made possible by the first. The steps for being filled by the Spirit should be followed carefully.

The most important step in being filled with the Spirit is the total commitment of your life to Christ. The self-life always causes depression. Making Christ Lord of your life each day enables you to avoid self-pity, self-indulgence, self-centeredness, and the many natural expressions of selfishness.

Who Controls Your Life?

It is not difficult to determine whether or not your life is committed to Christ at any given time. Just ask yourself, "Who is in control of my life right now?" The throne on the next page symbolizes the free will of man. Only one person can sit as Lord on the throne of your life at one time, you or Jesus Christ. The "S" on the throne of a carnal Christian represents his self. Christ is in his life but is not allowed to control it. Such living, which unfortunately is all too-common, constitutes a miserable state of existence. Christians who remain at the helm of their lives become unproductive and unattractive. Nothing about their lives exemplifies the change that Christ brings,

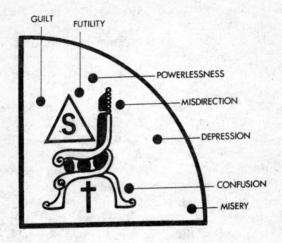

GUILT   FUTILITY

POWERLESSNESS

MISDIRECTION

DEPRESSION

CONFUSION

MISERY

S

CARNAL CHRISTIAN

for their self-directed program and ego-centered perspective belie their position as new creatures in Christ Jesus. Some would even dare to ask God's blessing upon their selfish designs, but this doesn't exempt them from misery and emptiness.

The Christ-controlled life steadily wins over depression. Jesus Christ, by His Holy Spirit, sits on the throne of this person's life, directing his thoughts, feelings and actions.

Life embraces an endless number of decisions, large and small. Where shall I live? What shall I pursue as a life vocation? Whom shall I marry? Either you or Jesus Christ will make these decisions. The life of faith and commitment to Christ places all decisions in His hands. The Bible

17

teaches, "In all thy ways acknowledge him, and he shall direct thy paths" (Prov. 3:6).

The illustration on the previous page describes that decision-making process with the following diagram and dots, each dot representing a decision in life.

The carnal Christian runs his own life and makes his own decisions, whereas the Christ-controlled Christian turns them over to Jesus Christ by prayerfully asking, "Lord Jesus, how do You want me to handle this situation?" "Do You want me to take this job opportunity?" "How do You want me to respond to my wife, or husband, or children, or boss, or neighbors?"

The practical differences in the two life styles are clearly listed in the above diagram. The self-controlled life is miserable. The Christ-controlled life is dynamic! One propagates disarray and confusion, inducing self to stagger from crisis to crisis. The Christ-controlled life guarantees peace and confidence, thus avoiding many crises (because it is supernaturally directed), and with confidence faces those inescapable crises as they come. This believer is confident that his Director will abundantly supply every need.

I had just come in from water skiing on San Diego Bay with my sons when we met a college student named Bill. He began to tell me what Christ meant to him personally and how He was controlling his entire life. Since I hadn't seen him in church for several weeks, I asked which church he was attending regularly. (I have found that

Christians cannot walk in the Spirit very long unless they go *regularly* to a Bible-teaching church where they can feed their mind, heart and spirit on the Word of God.) He replied, "Oh, I haven't been going anywhere lately." "What do you do on Sunday mornings, Bill?" He honestly replied, "I sleep in." "But I thought you were letting Jesus Christ control your life now." Rather peevishly he retorted, "I don't have to go to church to be a good Christian." "No," I said, "but if Jesus Christ is in control of your life at 9:30 on Sunday morning, what do you think He would have you do?" Then his subtle self-indulgent thought processes came to the fore. "Sunday is the only day I have to sleep in. I work and study hard all week long, and I think I deserve one day to relax and do my thing." When I confronted him with the fact that his excuse contained five personal pronouns and totally excluded Jesus Christ, he suddenly realized that he had never consulted Christ about his Sunday morning decision.

I had the advantage in that conversation because I already knew what Jesus Christ's decision would be. Hebrews 10:25 says, "Not forsaking the assembling of ourselves together, as the manner of some is; but exhorting one another: and so much the more, as you see the day approaching."

When confronted with any decision in life, prayerfully ask, "Lord Jesus, what about this?" Usually a verse of Scripture or a biblical principle will pop into your mind and cast light on the subject. If you act in that light, you will make a proper decision; if you don't, you will once again be thrown into the den of error. Never ask, "What do I want to do about this?" True spiritual maturity, the product of time spent in the Word and continuous walking in the Spirit, manifests itself when Christ's will and your will are synonymous.

Depression-prone people should scrutinize their thought processes to see if they are controlled by Jesus Christ. His control does not tolerate self-pitying thoughts, and consequently Christ-controlled living is depression-free living.

The Results of the Spirit-Filled Life

Though everyone wants the results of the Spirit-filled life, few people experience them. I have never met anyone who premeditatedly set out to make himself miserable, but most people do! By running their own lives selfishly, they create inordinate distress.

In this regard, Ephesians 5:18-21 becomes a crucial passage for Christians. It should be memorized and contemplated daily. After commanding us to be continually filled (or controlled) by the Holy Spirit, it specifies the results. Note them carefully:

Verse 19 — a song in your heart
Verse 20 — a thanksgiving attitude
Verse 21 — a submissive spirit

· You will never find a miserable person with a song in his heart, a thanksgiving attitude and a submissive spirit! Nor will you find a happy person without them. And isn't happiness what *everyone* wants out of life? Unfortunately, people try to achieve their happiness through the mental, emotional or physical areas of life, but it cannot be found there. Only by turning one's life and all of its decisions over to Christ can one ever gain lasting happiness!

(c) *Forgive those who sin against you!* — It is impossible to walk in the Spirit for a protracted period of time while refusing to obey Christ's command to "forgive those who trespass against you" (Matt. 6:12). Depressed-prone individuals are usually conscious of a loved one or relative who rejected or injured them earlier in life. Until they forgive that person, they will never know lasting victory over depression. In fact, they will never develop spiritual maturity either. Jesus said, "For if ye forgive men their trespasses, your heavenly Father will also forgive you: *But if ye forgive not men their trespasses, neither will your Father forgive your trespasses*" (Matt. 6:14, 15).

The unforgiving spirit of a carnal Christian is harmful spiritually, mentally, emotionally and physically. You have doubtless heard the expression, "He burns me up!" Little does a person realize that the bitterness festering in his mind will destroy his relationship with God and man.

An unforgiving attitude is never limited to one person. Like cancer in the body, it is a mental disease that feeds on itself until it severs the expression of love and other wholesome emotions. In addition, it makes an invalid of its subject, a prey to every gust of passion. Bitterness tends to expand and intensify through the years until even little things arouse his rancorous spirit. I have found that a bitter, unforgiving thought pattern toward someone you hate will even minimize or limit your expressions of love for someone you love.

If you would sincerely rid yourself of depression, ask yourself, "Is there anyone in life I have never forgiven?" If so, confess that sin to God immediately and ask God to take away that habit pattern. If the individual is aware of your resentment or bitterness, apologize personally if possible or by mail. Admittedly, this is a very difficult gesture, but it is essential for emotional stability.

A Christian couple came in for marriage counseling with several surface problems but no deep-rooted difficulties that I could find. In talking to the man, who seemed to be the primary source of friction in the home, I found that years before he had suffered a tragic experience with a business partner and had steadfastly harbored this affront and indulged in bitterness throughout the years. His resentful thinking pattern was not only a sin, but was also a mental habit pattern that spoiled his relationship with other people, including his wife. This bitterness was probably a major reason why the man had never become a mature and effective Christian. Finally recognizing his problem, he made an appointment with the man and asked his forgiveness. To his amazement, he found that eighteen months previously this man had become a Christian and had likewise been convicted about the matter. Today they are reasonably good friends, and a major source of irritation in the marriage of this couple has been removed. The elimination of that root of bitterness has improved his entire thinking pattern and strengthened his spiritual and emotional life to such a degree that business associates notice the change in him.

All causes of bitterness need not be real, but in some cases exist only in the imagination. One deeply depressed young woman came to me after an unhappy courtship explosion. As the author of the breakup, she concluded that she lacked a normal attitude toward the opposite sex. Sensing that it was abnormal to be so cold and indifferent to marriage, she came in for help. I understood enough about her background to know that she was raised by a divorced mother who sacrificed everything for her daughter during her childhood. When the girl was twelve her mother remarried a fine Christian man who adopted her as his own child and tried his best to raise her properly as a daughter.

This nineteen-year-old girl was consumed with a spirit of bitterness toward her loving and devoted mother because she "smothered and dominated my every decision." Unfortunately, the mother, blaming herself for the breakup of her first marriage, had bent over backwards to make it up to the daughter and consequently had become overprotective. (A parent raising children alone must realize that God is able to supply the needs of a child raised with only one parent in the home.) Some bright-eyed college sophomore with a psychology book under his arm informed her that she was overly dependent upon her mother. As a result she built up an artificial case of resentment until it spilled over and stifled her normal emotions toward others. Only by confessing her sins of resentment and ingratitude to God and by writing a letter of apology to her mother was she able to be restored spiritually, emotionally and mentally.

Someone has sagely remarked, "Forgive or perish." The human mind is so constructed that if you protract bitterness and hatred toward someone, it will ultimately destroy you.

(d) *Renew your mind daily* — As we have already seen, the way to consistently transform your life is to renew your mind with the Word of God. The way of this world is so contrary to the ways of God that it is nearly impossible to find any spiritual help in the secular world. Therefore, just as you nourish your body on a daily basis, you should feed your mind those things that will contribute to your spiritual development. All such wisdom comes from God and is found in His library of divine truth called the Holy Bible. Only by reading, studying, meditating, memorizing and hearing His wisdom will you become the mature Christian that God wants you to be, established in the faith and competent to overcome tendencies toward depression.

(e) *Practice creative imagery daily through prayer* — In chapter 11 of *How to Win Over Depression* [*] we examined the importance of fashioning a wholesome image of yourself and your goals on the screen of your imagination daily. This chapter should be studied carefully and put into daily practice by anyone with a tendency toward depression. If you have met the above conditions then you are now ready to follow these ten steps to victory over depression:

1. Accept yourself as a creature of God.

Thank God that you are an object of His love and that He made you as you are. Make a special point of thanking Him for whatever part of your nature or looks you are apt to regret. Since it is impossible to change, and since God controls the genes at conception, it is an act of disobedience to resent those areas of your life that cannot be changed. Thank Him for what you are and trust Him to gradually make you the person He wants you to be.

2. Accept God's forgiveness for your sins.

If you find sin in your life, of course, confess it. But whenever you examine

---

[*] See *How to Win Over Depression* by Tim LaHaye (Zondervan, 1974, Grand Rapids, Michigan).

yourself on the screen of your imagination, you will quite naturally focus upon the mistakes and sins of the past. Once having confessed them, be sure to thank God for His forgiveness. Accepting God's forgiveness would mean that you see yourself as clothed in the righteousness of Jesus, not in the raggedness of your sins. "He that overcometh, the same shall be clothed in white raiment; and I will not blot out his name out of the book of life, but I will confess his name before my Father, and before his angels" (Rev. 3:5).

3. Superimpose God onto your self-image.

Thank God for His presence in your life in a real and practical way, reminding yourself as did the Apostle Paul, "I *can* do all things *through Christ* which strengtheneth me" (Phil. 4:13).

4. Visualize yourself as God is shaping you.

Resist the temptation to see yourself in the light of failures past, but envision yourself as growing and maturing as both you and God desire you to be. One mother confined to a small home with three preschool children found this practice helpful in learning to control her temper. For some time she had viewed herself on the screen of her imagination as an ill-tempered, irrational mother gradually losing control of herself because of the heavy demands of her children. The more she saw herself in such a light, the more she acted this way. By visualizing herself daily as Christ would have her become, she gradually learned to respond more patiently and graciously in obedience to the Spirit's control of her life. Naturally, the more patience she actuated, the more she reinforced the positive image on the screen of her imagination. This in turn made it easier for her to be controlled and patient. The Bible tells us, "Let this mind be in you which is also in Christ Jesus." Think of yourself as a reflection of the mind of Christ. How would He treat children under those circumstances? Or how would He respond to an irate boss or a demanding, domineering parent? See yourself reacting as Christ would and you will find yourself gradually sustaining that reaction.

5. **Visualize by faith your basic life goals and write them down.**

By noting your objectives and writing them down, you activate your subconscious mind to remind you of those things needing to be done in order to fulfill your goals. By praying about them in faith, you also summon the power of God on your behalf, which makes it possible to achieve the impossible.

6. Always be positive.

There is no place in the Christian's life for negativism. Linked as we are with the divine power of God, we should never anticipate anything but success. Avoid the complainer, the griper and the critic; most of all, avoid imitating them. The personnel director of a large corporation who had learned the powerful influence of negativism on people explained to me why he selected one particular man over another for a special job assignment. I knew both men and volunteered my surprise at his selection, for I felt that the man he passed over was the more effective employee. He responded, "I never hire a top echelon executive until I first interview his wife. Although I am aware of the tremendous capabilities of our mutual friend, I am also conscious of the excessive griping habits to which his wife is given. I therefore conclude that she would have a harmful, de-motivating influence on his work. I chose the other man because I judged that the margin between them would easily be bridged by the supportive role of his wife."

Negativism, pessimism, griping, criticism and gossip are not only harmful but also contagious. In fact, you reinforce them in your own mind every time you verbalize them. Keep your conversation *and* your mind positive at all times. Listen to the most powerful instruction on this subject in Scripture: "Finally, brethren, whatsoever things are true, whatsoever things are honest, whatsoever things are just, whatsoever things are pure, whatsoever things are lovely, whatsoever things are of good report; if there be any virtue, and if there be any praise, think on these things" (Phil. 4:8).

7. Anticipate the superabundant life God has in store for you.

God has fashioned a complete plan for your life, but it is flexible. It includes the good, acceptable and perfect will of God. Romans 12:1 says, "I beseech you therefore, brethren, by the mercies of God, that ye present your bodies a living sacrifice, holy, acceptable unto God, which is your reasonable service."

Man's Needs   *Man's Desires*

"My God shall
supply all your need"

"That your joy
may be full"

God's Abundance

"Exceeding abundantly above
all you can ask or think."

"According to your faith be it unto you"

We read in Philippians 4:19, "But my God shall supply all your need according to his riches in glory by Christ Jesus." Concerning His desire to supply your wholesome, God-honoring wants, John 16:24 promises, "Hitherto have ye asked nothing in my name: ask, and ye shall receive, that your joy may be full." In addition, He desires to shower you "exceeding abundantly above all" that you could ever ask or think (Eph. 3:20).

Most Christians spend their lives on the left-hand portion of the chart, asking God to supply their needs. I never *ask* Him to supply my need because He has already promised to do that. Years ago I found in John 16:24 that God loves to make me happy by supplying those things that I want and providing these wants in accord with His basic plan for my life. In more recent years, I have found that God is a Father who enjoys giving to His children. In fact, Jesus Christ compared an earthly father with the heavenly Father when He said, "If ye then, being evil, know how to give good gifts unto your children, *how much more*

30

shall your Father which is in heaven give good things to them that ask him?" (Matt. 7:11).

One day after a wonderful Christmas at our home, it dawned on me that it is thrilling and satisfying to be a parent. We have always received much pleasure and enjoyment in giving to our children, even in excess of their wants. Most parents are like that. We don't give because they deserve it, because most children today already possess more than they deserve. Rather, we parents give to our children purely because we love them. If that is true of us, how much more is it true of God! He wants to give you "exceeding abundantly above all that we ask or think"! Never limit God by unbelief, but anticipate that He will perform something supernatural in your life. Remember, "According to your faith be it unto you." Your success does not depend on your opportunity or ability, but on your faith. If your faith is weak, ask God to grant you more faith that you in turn may anticipate the power of a supernatural and superabundant God working in your life.

8. Seek first the kingdom of God.

Matthew 6:33 makes it clear that the Christian can make no allowance for greed or self-motive in his life. Although he may seek employment or material gain, he can never let it become his primary objective. Instead, his first objective should be to seek the kingdom of God and His righteousness.

Any time our quest for material gain runs contrary to the kingdom of God or His righteousness, it is wrong for us. Even if we were successful in achieving some degree of prosperity while doing something contrary to the will of God, it would not be a lasting source of enjoyment. Remember, it is essential that you be obedient to God. In establishing your priorities, consider the first commandment, "Thou shalt love the Lord thy God with all thy heart, soul, and mind." You can judge your sincere love for God by whether or not you serve Him. If your first objective is to earn a living and to stockpile this world's goods, then you not only demonstrate your greed, but also a lack of sufficient love for God. Give God His rightful place in your heart, express it in your attitude toward things, and He will bless you with items you need, provisions "exceeding abundantly above all that you ask or think."

9. Give yourself to God to serve people.

The most rewarding and gratifying experiences in life come in serving people. This will be emotionally therapeutic. Depressed people are inclined to spend too much time thinking about themselves. Serving God by helping people forces you to think about someone besides yourself. I am personally convinced that God has oriented the human psyche in such a way that unless a man befriends others, he cannot be satisfied with himself. The rewards of such service are not only beneficial for eternity, but also helpful in this life.

One seriously depressed woman decided that she had never really helped anyone since her children went off to school. Although she had taught Sunday school in her earlier years, the birth of three small children directed her energies elsewhere. When she was free during the day, she considered it essential to "rest up," but finally she was overcome by depression. As we talked, she realized it was time for her to recognize that God could use her as a means of reaching her neighbors for Christ, so she started a women's Bible class on Wednesdays. Several weeks later she had become a very dynamic, outgoing woman. While visiting casually at a social activity, I smilingly inquired, "How is your depression lately?" I shall never forget her response. She laughed aloud, and with a twinkle in her eye said, "I don't have time to be depressed anymore!" The fact that several of her neighbors had found Christ and two families were spared a disastrous breakup in their marriages had given her a new purpose for living and a sense of self-esteem.

The Bible teaches, "Give, and it shall be given unto you; good measure, pressed down, and shaken together, and running over, shall men give into your bosom. For with the same measure that ye mete withal it shall be measured to you again" (Luke 6:38). Scripture also promises, "He that findeth his life shall lose it: and he that loseth his life for my sake shall find it" (Matt. 10:39). If you would really live free from depression, stop hoarding your life and give it away.

10. In everything give thanks.

> "In every thing give thanks: for this is the will of God in Christ Jesus concerning you" (1 Thess. 5:18). That verse offers an absolute guarantee against emotional depression! For several years in family conferences before thousands of people I have announced, "I can give you a money-back guarantee that will keep you from ever being depressed again. It is found in 1 Thessalonians 5:18." So far I have not encountered a single exception. There is just no way a healthy person filled with the Holy Spirit, rendering thanks in everything, can become depressed.

In recent years I have noted a new emphasis upon this matter of giving thanks that has injected lasting joy into the lives of millions of Christians. We may approach thanksgiving in two contrasting ways: consciously by sight or consciously by faith. Consider them individually:

(a) *Give thanks consciously by sight* — The Bible repeatedly advises gratitude as the ideal mental attitude. A grateful person is a happy person. Counting our many blessings to see what God has already done in our lives develops an optimistic faith to trust Him for the future.

Depressed people are usually ungrateful people who in turn become unhappy people. I have found it therapeutic to ask such people to list those things for which they are grateful and review this record once or twice a day, thanking God in prayer for these blessings. The results are absolutely amazing. Some counselees have been so morose and unappreciative that I have actually had to help them work up their list. But once it was made, they began to catch the spirit of praise and dis-

---

A note from . . .

PASTOR TIM LAHAYE

The problem is that almost universal human response is to feel sorry for oneself whenever an adverse situation occurs. Then the individual indulges in the mental sin of self-pity. In my opinion, nothing is more emotionally or mentally destructive than the thinking pattern of self-pity, not to mention the spiritual poverty it causes. The only way to avoid that is through the thinking pattern of thanksgiving and that requires being filled with and walking in the Spirit (Gal. 5:16).

cover far more to be grateful for than they had realized. Rehearsing objects of thanksgiving consistently for one week revitalized their mental attitudes and dispelled all sorrow and despondence.

(b) *Consciously give thanks by faith* — At times in life it is impossible to understand God's dealings with us, usually because we lack the divine perspective. God sees not only the present circumstances but also the end result, extending His provision on a long-term, permanent basis. Unfortunately, we are usually more concerned with the immediate and, consequently, when circumstances annoy or displease us, we are prone to gripe mentally rather than "give thanks in everything." For that reason it is essential that we learn to give thanks by faith.

We have already seen that our computer-like mind will reject the impossible. Humanly speaking, giving thanks "in everything" is unreasonable and inconceivable, a violation of logic. For that reason we must learn to program God into the situation and recognize that He has a plan, including even the most unhappy circumstances which work for our long-range good. Therefore, as an expression of our faith and confidence in His love and ability to act in our behalf, we should "in everything give thanks, for this is the will of God in Christ Jesus concerning you."

THANKSGIVING AS A HABIT

Just as we form bad habits, we also create good habits. Most of us brush our teeth every day, not because we enjoy the process, but because we recognize its value. Consequently we have developed the habit. By the same token we can create the good habit of giving thanks in everything in obedience to the will of God. Refusal to be obedient in this regard can make you depressed at almost a moment's notice, because the unexpected circumstances of life are bound to strike at the most inopportune time. If you react negatively, you will experience emotional depression and become spiritually useless to God at that precise moment.

Lest you think these are idle words and not genuine experience, let me share with you my own predicament as I write these words. In twenty-five years I had never missed a preaching assignment, although I have had some close calls. At 11:50 this particular morning I completed a pastor's seminar in Amarillo, Texas. Seated on a Continental Airlines 727, I was expecting to arrive in Dallas at 2:20 and catch a 3:00 flight to Atlanta, Georgia, where I was to begin a Family Life Seminar at 7:00 P.M. At 12:55, as we were taxiing out to the run-up area, I watched the pilot suddenly turn the plane around and head back to the landing station. A few moments later I saw him deplane, meet with a mechanic and begin taking the cover off one of the engines. Subsequently a thirty-minute delay was announced. A few minutes later the mechanic brought a piece of cable out of the engine, held it up and gave the pilot a message. Within a few seconds I heard over the P.A. system that a defective part would have to be replaced and that the flight was cancelled.

Walking inside the air terminal, I practiced what I have just written. "Praise the Lord." God knew that the next flight from Amarillo to Dallas arrived eleven minutes after the Dallas to Atlanta flight. When this information was confirmed, I asked Him for guidance and then called an air charter service at another airport. The pilot assured me that for $200 I could be flown privately to Dallas and arrive on time. Although I thoroughly enjoyed the flight, we landed just as my Delta flight lifted off the runway at Love Field. "Now what am I going to do?" I knew the choice was mine. I could grumble, be miserable, or praise the Lord and just let Him take care of the details. So I decided to take the biblical course. I sat down, finishing this chapter.

The Director of Family Life Seminars had me paged over the loudspeaker system. After I informed him that I could not get into Atlanta until 9:30 that night, fifteen minutes *after* the seminar concluded, he asked, "What am I going to do?" "Why not praise the Lord?" As I write this, I am fully conscious that some rather irate Atlantans probably attended our seminar, but I can expect the heavenly Father to provide for their needs in ways I do not have any manner of foreseeing. Of one thing I am certain: I had done the will of God to the best of my ability, I had faced uncontrollable circumstances with joy, and I could therefore sit back without worry or agitation, trusting Him to work out the details. Doubtless He has something in mind in this experience that I know nothing about.

As I walked by the ticket counter and heard the angry passengers berating the ticket agent, I couldn't help but think, "Why can't everyone learn the secret of living by faith, that they too might 'in everything give thanks'?" The day may come when I will understand by sight the delay and the suspended engagement, but then again, I may not. Of one thing I am certain: shrill lamentations and prayers of protestation, which would reflect my natural temperament tendency, will not help a bit. At a time like this a succinct biblical principle encourages me: "My times are in thy hand" (Ps. 31:15). Whatever His reason for wanting me to miss that flight, I can trust Him to know what is best for me. *

Are You a Groaner or a Praiser?

My friend Ken Poure, who has been greatly used of God in family conferences throughout the nation, suggests that our reaction at times like this exhibits our spiritual maturity. He proposes that

---

* For the curious, that night the F. L. S. Director shared two Family Life films by Dr. Henry Brandt which really met the needs of the people. When I began the following morning, they were in an excellent mood and we enjoyed an exciting seminar. Had I resorted to worry, agitation, or anxiety while waiting in Dallas, it would obviously have been an exercise in futility. God knows what He is doing!

the time lapse between one's knowledge of a disappointing experience and his praising the Lord by faith will reveal the strength of his spiritual life. If you can rejoice in a matter of moments, you are spiritual. If it takes you fifteen minutes to an hour, you are still growing. If an hour or several days pass, "you are in real trouble," Ken warns. Then he asks a very perceptive question: "Are you a praiser or a groaner?" Most people are one or the other. The sooner you learn to praise God in the face of adverse circumstances or frustrated expectations, the happier you will be and the more you will live a depression-free life.

If you are interested in further exploring the problem of depression, you would profit from reading Dr. LaHaye's book, *How to Win Over Depression*, which includes chapters on:

The Problem of Depression
Struggles Against Depression
The Symptoms of Depression
The Cycles of Depression
The Causes of Depression
Is There a Cure for Depression?
The Place of Anger in Depression
Self-Pity and Depression
How to Overcome Self-Pity
Depression and Your Mind
Depression and Your Self-Image
Depression and Your Temperament
Depression and the Occult
Depression and Music
Ten Steps to Victory Over Depression
How to Help Your Children
    Avoid Depression
How to Help a Depressed Friend
The Miserable Majority
An Eighty-Five-Year-Old Optimist

ORDER

Tim LaHaye

BESTSELLERS

☐	The Act of Marriage	Large Paper	**$4.95**
☐	The Act of Marriage	Pocket Book	**$2.95**
☐	How to Win Over Depression	Large Paper	**$4.95**
☐	How to Win Over Depression	Pocket Book	**$2.95**
☐	Revelation — Illustrated & Made Plain	Large Paper	**$6.95**
☐	Ten Steps to Victory Over Depression	Pocket Book	**$ .95**

Please send me the books I have checked above. I am enclosing $ _____ (please add $1.00 to cover postage and handling). Send check or money order—no cash or C.O.D's please.

Mr./Mrs./Miss _____

Address _____

City _____ State _____ Zip _____

Please allow 3 weeks for delivery.

Zondervan Retail Marketing Services. 1420 Robinson Rd., S.E. Grand Rapids, MI 49506

Prices subject to change without notice

Buy them at your local bookstore or use this handy coupon for ordering: